THIS BOOK BELONGS TO

START DATE

HEAVEN AND EARTH
WILL PASS AWAY, BUT MY
WORDS WILL NOT PASS
AWAY.

MATTHEW 24:35

A

take up & READ

PUBLICATION

Managing Editor: Elizabeth Foss

Copy Editor: Rosie Hill

Design by: Kristin Foss

ISBN-13: 978-1987579277

ISBN-10: 1987579275

VISIT US

takeupandread.org

BE SOCIAL

Facebook @takeupandread

Instagram @takeupandread

Twitter @totakeupandread

SEND A NOTE

totakeupandread@gmail.com

CONNECT

#TakeUpAndRead

HOW TO USE THIS BOOK

This journal was created for you to use on your own as you study God's Word. We want to help you connect meaningfully with Scripture in prayer, and then give you tools to stay connected throughout your day. The intentionally open-ended design invites you to make this your own. Begin with Lectio Divina (Holy Reading). If you are new to Lectio Divina or need fresh inspiration, read our introductory essay for a brief history and some practical pointers. Please enjoy this fresh design and original artwork as you pray the Scriptures every day.

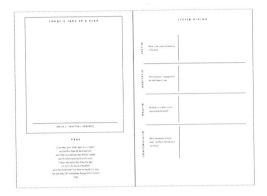

DAILY SCRIPTURE READING

Follow our Bible reading plans online or create your own. Use this space to write the Word.

LECTIO DIVINA

Immerse yourself in a multi-faceted, prayerful study of the text. For help with historical context to better complete the first box, consult a study Bible and/or and a Bible dictionary.

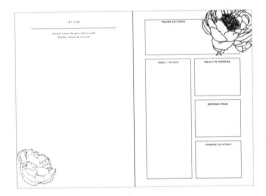

ACTIO

Listen to the promptings of the Holy Spirit, and let the Word inspire your actions. There is room here for menu plans, home-keeping notes, and even a place for an intentional plan to care for yourself—every day.

WEEKLY SCRIPTURE VERSE

You can find a weekly memory verse in the Take Up & Read Bible reading plans. If you are studying on your own, challenge yourself each week to memorize a verse or two.

At Take Up & Read, we want you to discover what prompts and pages are most useful to you. There is no perfect way to perform lectio—the important thing is that you take the time to have a conversation with God, using His Word as your guide.

LECTIO PAGE IN ACTION

2 Timothy 3:16-17

What is the objective meaning of the text?

Written by Paul who was in prison to Timothy who was in Ephesus. "All Scripture" means what we know as the OT. But also might include early gospel accounts that later became the NT.

What personal message does the text have for me?

The social media feeds I choose can compete w/the message of the gospel. Scripture can always be trusted. It should be my inspiration when preparing for everything — my go-to instead of the internet.

What do I say to the Lord in response to His word?

Thank you for giving me your Word. Remind me throughout my day, when I lose my way and look to other sources of direction that You have everything I need to do Your good work.

What conversion of mind, heart, and life is He asking of me today?

I think God is reminding me to get the ratio right: consult Scripture more than other things that compete for my time & attention.

LECTIO DIVINA

Together, as a community of faithful women, we endeavor to better understand the heart of the gospel and to live it out in our lives. Each day, we invite our souls to encounter our Lord.

How? How will the tired soul living in the woman in the midst of secular culture and busyness still herself and find her Lord? How will she find hope and new energy in the act of one more thing on her to-do list?

She will pray—more. That's right. She will take more time to pray even though so many things pull on her time. Can we do that together? Can we take up for ourselves the ancient tradition of lectio divina and let the Word lead us to live in charity? We can and we must. This is the best way to prepare ourselves for each day with peaceful composure and serene grace.

In his 2010 apostolic exhortation *Verbum Domini*, Pope Benedict XVI beautifully instructs the faithful to prayerfully read the Scripture. Following his lead, we will be drawn into a practice that is as old as Scripture itself. We will closely read and ponder Scripture passages carefully chosen for this season.

In the early Christian communities, Scripture was read to nourish faith with the wisdom of truth. When we hold the New Testament, we take up the understanding that the first Christians had of the Old Testament, together with the divine revelation the Holy Spirit granted to Jesus' earliest followers.

The Church Fathers' faith was informed by their careful, prayerful reading of the Word. Today, we are blessed to welcome their wisdom into our reading when we access the commentaries that were the fruit of their lectio. The monastic movement grew in the fertile soil of lectio divina. The daily, ordered life of the monks was (and is) centered upon spiritual reading of Scripture. Can ordinary women in the twenty-first century find spiritual nourishment and new life in this age-old practice of holy men?

We can.

There are five steps in the pattern, five distinct movements that will direct the way we travel through our days. First, we read. Then, a meditation engages the mind, using reason to search for knowledge in the message. The prayer is the movement of the heart towards God, a beseeching on behalf of the soul. The contemplation elevates the mind and suspends it in God's presence. Finally, the action is the way we live our lives as a gift of charity towards others. It's a tall order, but it's the very best way to live.

Let's take a careful look at each step.

Pope Benedict writes, "It opens with the reading (lectio) of a text, which leads to a desire to understand its true content: what does the biblical text say in itself." (*Verbum Domini*, 87) This is where we explore the literary genre of the text, the characters we meet in the story, and the objective meaning intended by the author. We usually offer several passages which work together towards a common theme; you can choose just one passage, or you can look at the group together, as the Holy Spirit inspires. A good study Bible and/or a Bible dictionary will help you to place the reading in context.

"Next comes meditation (meditatio), which asks: what does the biblical text say to us?" (DV, 87) Prayerfully we ponder what personal message the text holds for each of us and what effect that message should have on our lives.

"Following this comes prayer (oratio), which asks the question: what do we say to the Lord in response to his word? Prayer, as petition, intercession, thanksgiving and praise, is the primary way by which the word transforms us." (DV, 87) What do we say to God in response to His Word? We ask Him what He desires of us. We ask Him for the strength and grace to do His will. Moved by His mercy, we give Him thanks and praise.

The fourth act is "contemplation (contemplatio), during which we take up, as a gift from God, His own way of seeing and judging reality, and ask ourselves what conversion of mind, heart and life is the Lord asking of us?" (DV, 87) Here, reflect on how God has conveyed His love for us in the day's Scripture. Recognize the beauty of His gifts and the goodness of His mercy and rest in that. Let God light you from within and look out on the world in a new way because you have been transformed by the process of prayerful Scripture study.

Finally, the whole point of this time we've taken from our day is to get up from the reading and go live the gospel. Actio is where we make an act of our wills and resolve to bring the text to life in our lives.

This is our fiat.

The process of lectio divina is not concluded until it arrives at action (actio), which moves the believer to make his or her life a gift for others in charity. We find the supreme synthesis and fulfillment of this process in the Mother of God. For every member of the faithful Mary is the model of docile acceptance of God's word, for she "kept all these things, pondering them in her heart."(Lk 2:19; cf. 2:51) (DV, 87)

As a community at Take Up & Read, we will endeavor to engage in lectio divina every day. To correlate with each day's Scripture passages, we've created pages for your time of prayer, and we've created pages for your active time. We want this book to come alive in your hands, to bring you a spiritual springtime. Try to take the time each day to dig deep, but if you have to cut your time short, don't be discouraged. Ask the Blessed Mother to help you find pockets throughout the day to re-engage. You don't have to fill in every box. There is no right or wrong answer. And you don't have to dig deeply with every passage.

Pray the parts you can, and trust the Holy Spirit to water it well in your soul. Know that God can do loaves and fishes miracles with your small parcels of time, if only you are willing to offer Him what you have. Before your days—and then your weeks—get swallowed with the ordinary to-do lists of life's hustle, sit in prayer and see how you can tune your heart to the beat of the Lord's, and ensure that the best gift you give is your life, poured out for others in charity.

NOTES

DAY ONE

DATE:

SCRIPTURE MEMORY COPY

BOOK | CHAPTER | VERSE(S)

WEEKLY SCRIPTURE MEMORY

HIDE IT IN YOUR HEART

When we memorize Scripture, we imitate Jesus, who hid God's Word in His heart and who proclaimed it even in His most sorrowful agony. As He hung in the final moments of His life, Scripture was the last thing on His breath, and Jesus, "crying with a loud voice, said, 'Father, into your hands I commend my spirit.' Having said this, He breathed his last." (Luke 23:46) We can almost certainly know that Jesus learned those words (from Psalm 31) from His mother as a prayer when He was a little boy. She poured into Him a treasury of Scripture and He knew just where to find it all His life.

To hold the Word so close and so dear that it is what sustains us in the very last moments of our life! To hide the Lord in our hearts in such a real and present way that He spills out into our speech when we are neediest and when we are most joyful! These are the true goals of the Take Up & Read studies.

We invite you to use the verses we've chosen in our online Bible reading plans, or to listen to the inspiration of the Holy Spirit and select verses of your own to memorize.

TODAY'S TAKE UP & READ

BOOK | CHAPTER | VERSE(S)

PRAY

Come Holy Spirit, fill the hearts of your faithful
and kindle in them the fire of your love.
Send forth your Spirit and they shall be created.
And You shall renew the face of the earth.
O God, who by the light of the Holy Spirit,
did instruct the hearts of the faithful,
grant that by the same Holy Spirit we may be truly wise
and ever enjoy His consolations, Through Christ Our Lord,
Amen.

LECTIO DIVINA

LECTIO

What is the objective meaning
of the text?

MEDITATIO

What personal message does
the text have for me?

ORATIO

What do I say to the Lord in
response to His word?

CONTEMPLATIO

What conversion of mind,
heart, and life is He asking of
me today?

ACTIO

How will I make my life a gift for others in charity?
What does God want me to do today?

PRAYER PETITIONS

TASKS + TO DOS

MEALS TO NOURISH

KEEPING HOME

KINDNESS TO MYSELF

How did I progress in living the Word today?

"And when night comes, and you look back over the day and see how fragmentary everything has been, and how much you planned that has gone undone, and all the reasons you have to be embarrassed and ashamed: just take everything exactly as it is, put it in God's hands and leave it with Him. Then you will be able to rest in Him — really rest — and start the next day as a new life."
— St. Teresa Benedicta of the Cross (Edith Stein)

DAY TWO

DATE:

BOOK | CHAPTER | VERSE(S)

PRAY

Come Holy Spirit, fill the hearts of your faithful
and kindle in them the fire of your love.
Send forth your Spirit and they shall be created.
And You shall renew the face of the earth.
O God, who by the light of the Holy Spirit,
did instruct the hearts of the faithful,
grant that by the same Holy Spirit we may be truly wise
and ever enjoy His consolations, Through Christ Our Lord,
Amen.

LECTIO DIVINA

LECTIO

What is the objective meaning
of the text?

MEDITATIO

What personal message does
the text have for me?

ORATIO

What do I say to the Lord in
response to His word?

CONTEMPLATIO

What conversion of mind,
heart, and life is He asking of
me today?

A C T I O

How will I make my life a gift for others in charity?

What does God want me to do today?

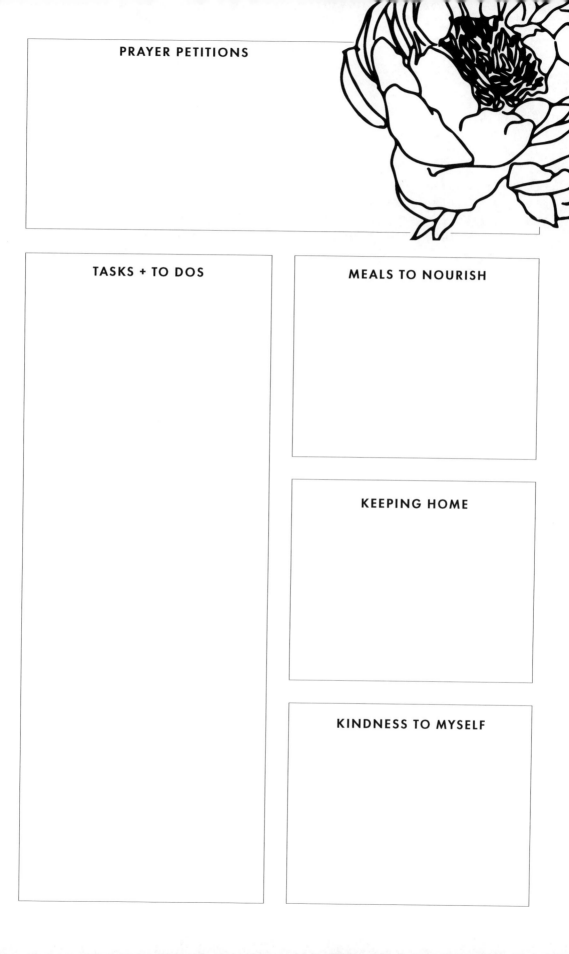

PRAYER PETITIONS

TASKS + TO DOS

MEALS TO NOURISH

KEEPING HOME

KINDNESS TO MYSELF

How did I progress in living the Word today?

"And when night comes, and you look back over the day and see how fragmentary everything has been, and how much you planned that has gone undone, and all the reasons you have to be embarrassed and ashamed: just take everything exactly as it is, put it in God's hands and leave it with Him. Then you will be able to rest in Him — really rest — and start the next day as a new life."
— St. Teresa Benedicta of the Cross (Edith Stein)

DAY THREE

DATE:

BOOK | CHAPTER | VERSE(S)

PRAY

*Come Holy Spirit, fill the hearts of your faithful
and kindle in them the fire of your love.
Send forth your Spirit and they shall be created.
And You shall renew the face of the earth.
O God, who by the light of the Holy Spirit,
did instruct the hearts of the faithful,
grant that by the same Holy Spirit we may be truly wise
and ever enjoy His consolations, Through Christ Our Lord,
Amen.*

LECTIO DIVINA

LECTIO

What is the objective meaning of the text?

MEDITATIO

What personal message does the text have for me?

ORATIO

What do I say to the Lord in response to His word?

CONTEMPLATIO

What conversion of mind, heart, and life is He asking of me today?

ACTIO

How will I make my life a gift for others in charity?
What does God want me to do today?

PRAYER PETITIONS

TASKS + TO DOS

MEALS TO NOURISH

KEEPING HOME

KINDNESS TO MYSELF

How did I progress in living the Word today?

"And when night comes, and you look back over the day and see how fragmentary everything has been, and how much you planned that has gone undone, and all the reasons you have to be embarrassed and ashamed: just take everything exactly as it is, put it in God's hands and leave it with Him. Then you will be able to rest in Him — really rest — and start the next day as a new life."
— St. Teresa Benedicta of the Cross (Edith Stein)

DAY FOUR

DATE:

TODAY'S TAKE UP & READ

BOOK | CHAPTER | VERSE(S)

PRAY

Come Holy Spirit, fill the hearts of your faithful
and kindle in them the fire of your love.
Send forth your Spirit and they shall be created.
And You shall renew the face of the earth.
O God, who by the light of the Holy Spirit,
did instruct the hearts of the faithful,
grant that by the same Holy Spirit we may be truly wise
and ever enjoy His consolations, Through Christ Our Lord,
Amen.

LECTIO DIVINA

LECTIO

What is the objective meaning
of the text?

MEDITATIO

What personal message does
the text have for me?

ORATIO

What do I say to the Lord in
response to His word?

CONTEMPLATIO

What conversion of mind,
heart, and life is He asking of
me today?

How will I make my life a gift for others in charity?

What does God want me to do today?

PRAYER PETITIONS

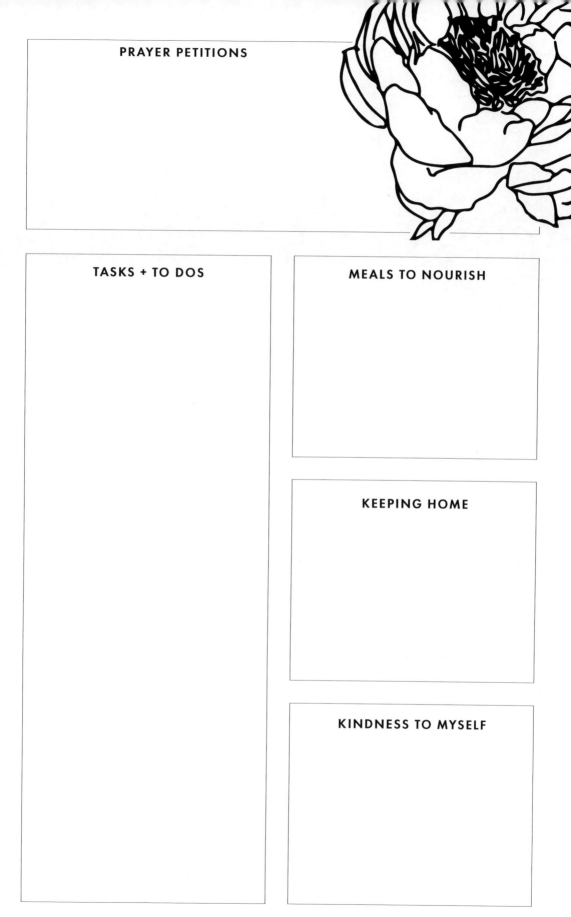

TASKS + TO DOS

MEALS TO NOURISH

KEEPING HOME

KINDNESS TO MYSELF

How did I progress in living the Word today?

"And when night comes, and you look back over the day and see how fragmentary everything has been, and how much you planned that has gone undone, and all the reasons you have to be embarrassed and ashamed: just take everything exactly as it is, put it in God's hands and leave it with Him. Then you will be able to rest in Him — really rest — and start the next day as a new life."
— St. Teresa Benedicta of the Cross (Edith Stein)

DAY FIVE

DATE:

BOOK | CHAPTER | VERSE(S)

PRAY

Come Holy Spirit, fill the hearts of your faithful
and kindle in them the fire of your love.
Send forth your Spirit and they shall be created.
And You shall renew the face of the earth.
O God, who by the light of the Holy Spirit,
did instruct the hearts of the faithful,
grant that by the same Holy Spirit we may be truly wise
and ever enjoy His consolations, Through Christ Our Lord,
Amen.

LECTIO DIVINA

LECTIO

What is the objective meaning of the text?

MEDITATIO

What personal message does the text have for me?

ORATIO

What do I say to the Lord in response to His word?

CONTEMPLATIO

What conversion of mind, heart, and life is He asking of me today?

ACTIO

How will I make my life a gift for others in charity?

What does God want me to do today?

PRAYER PETITIONS

TASKS + TO DOS

MEALS TO NOURISH

KEEPING HOME

KINDNESS TO MYSELF

How did I progress in living the Word today?

"And when night comes, and you look back over the day and see how fragmentary everything has been, and how much you planned that has gone undone, and all the reasons you have to be embarrassed and ashamed: just take everything exactly as it is, put it in God's hands and leave it with Him. Then you will be able to rest in Him — really rest — and start the next day as a new life." — St. Teresa Benedicta of the Cross (Edith Stein)

DAY SIX

DATE:

BOOK | CHAPTER | VERSE(S)

PRAY

*Come Holy Spirit, fill the hearts of your faithful
and kindle in them the fire of your love.
Send forth your Spirit and they shall be created.
And You shall renew the face of the earth.
O God, who by the light of the Holy Spirit,
did instruct the hearts of the faithful,
grant that by the same Holy Spirit we may be truly wise
and ever enjoy His consolations, Through Christ Our Lord,
Amen.*

LECTIO DIVINA

LECTIO

What is the objective meaning
of the text?

MEDITATIO

What personal message does
the text have for me?

ORATIO

What do I say to the Lord in
response to His word?

CONTEMPLATIO

What conversion of mind,
heart, and life is He asking of
me today?

ACTIO

How will I make my life a gift for others in charity?
What does God want me to do today?

PRAYER PETITIONS

TASKS + TO DOS

MEALS TO NOURISH

KEEPING HOME

KINDNESS TO MYSELF

How did I progress in living the Word today?

"And when night comes, and you look back over the day and see how fragmentary everything has been, and how much you planned that has gone undone, and all the reasons you have to be embarrassed and ashamed: just take everything exactly as it is, put it in God's hands and leave it with Him. Then you will be able to rest in Him — really rest — and start the next day as a new life."
— St. Teresa Benedicta of the Cross (Edith Stein)

DAY SEVEN

DATE:

BOOK | CHAPTER | VERSE(S)

PRAY

Come Holy Spirit, fill the hearts of your faithful
and kindle in them the fire of your love.
Send forth your Spirit and they shall be created.
And You shall renew the face of the earth.
O God, who by the light of the Holy Spirit,
did instruct the hearts of the faithful,
grant that by the same Holy Spirit we may be truly wise
and ever enjoy His consolations, Through Christ Our Lord,
Amen.

LECTIO DIVINA

LECTIO

What is the objective meaning of the text?

MEDITATIO

What personal message does the text have for me?

ORATIO

What do I say to the Lord in response to His word?

CONTEMPLATIO

What conversion of mind, heart, and life is He asking of me today?

ACTIO

How will I make my life a gift for others in charity?

What does God want me to do today?

PRAYER PETITIONS

TASKS + TO DOS

MEALS TO NOURISH

KEEPING HOME

KINDNESS TO MYSELF

How did I progress in living the Word today?

"And when night comes, and you look back over the day and see how fragmentary everything has been, and how much you planned that has gone undone, and all the reasons you have to be embarrassed and ashamed: just take everything exactly as it is, put it in God's hands and leave it with Him. Then you will be able to rest in Him — really rest — and start the next day as a new life." — St. Teresa Benedicta of the Cross (Edith Stein)

DAY EIGHT

DATE:

WEEKLY SCRIPTURE MEMORY

When we memorize Scripture, we imitate Jesus, who hid God's Word in His heart and who proclaimed it even in His most sorrowful agony. As He hung in the final moments of His life, Scripture was the last thing on His breath, and Jesus, "crying with a loud voice, said, 'Father, into your hands I commend my spirit.' Having said this, He breathed his last." (Luke 23:46) We can almost certainly know that Jesus learned those words (from Psalm 31) from His mother as a prayer when He was a little boy. She poured into Him a treasury of Scripture and He knew just where to find it all His life.

To hold the Word so close and so dear that it is what sustains us in the very last moments of our life! To hide the Lord in our hearts in such a real and present way that He spills out into our speech when we are neediest and when we are most joyful! These are the true goals of the Take Up & Read studies.

We invite you to use the verses we've chosen in our online Bible reading plans, or to listen to the inspiration of the Holy Spirit and select verses of your own to memorize.

TODAY'S TAKE UP & READ

BOOK | CHAPTER | VERSE(S)

PRAY

Come Holy Spirit, fill the hearts of your faithful
and kindle in them the fire of your love.
Send forth your Spirit and they shall be created.
And You shall renew the face of the earth.
O God, who by the light of the Holy Spirit,
did instruct the hearts of the faithful,
grant that by the same Holy Spirit we may be truly wise
and ever enjoy His consolations, Through Christ Our Lord,
Amen.

LECTIO DIVINA

LECTIO

What is the objective meaning
of the text?

MEDITATIO

What personal message does
the text have for me?

ORATIO

What do I say to the Lord in
response to His word?

CONTEMPLATIO

What conversion of mind,
heart, and life is He asking of
me today?

How will I make my life a gift for others in charity?

What does God want me to do today?

PRAYER PETITIONS

TASKS + TO DOS

MEALS TO NOURISH

KEEPING HOME

KINDNESS TO MYSELF

How did I progress in living the Word today?

"And when night comes, and you look back over the day and see how fragmentary everything has been, and how much you planned that has gone undone, and all the reasons you have to be embarrassed and ashamed: just take everything exactly as it is, put it in God's hands and leave it with Him. Then you will be able to rest in Him — really rest — and start the next day as a new life."
— St. Teresa Benedicta of the Cross (Edith Stein)

DAY NINE

DATE:

BOOK | CHAPTER | VERSE(S)

PRAY

Come Holy Spirit, fill the hearts of your faithful
and kindle in them the fire of your love.
Send forth your Spirit and they shall be created.
And You shall renew the face of the earth.
O God, who by the light of the Holy Spirit,
did instruct the hearts of the faithful,
grant that by the same Holy Spirit we may be truly wise
and ever enjoy His consolations, Through Christ Our Lord,
Amen.

LECTIO DIVINA

LECTIO

What is the objective meaning of the text?

MEDITATIO

What personal message does the text have for me?

ORATIO

What do I say to the Lord in response to His word?

CONTEMPLATIO

What conversion of mind, heart, and life is He asking of me today?

ACTIO

How will I make my life a gift for others in charity?
What does God want me to do today?

PRAYER PETITIONS

TASKS + TO DOS

MEALS TO NOURISH

KEEPING HOME

KINDNESS TO MYSELF

How did I progress in living the Word today?

"And when night comes, and you look back over the day and see how fragmentary everything has been, and how much you planned that has gone undone, and all the reasons you have to be embarrassed and ashamed: just take everything exactly as it is, put it in God's hands and leave it with Him. Then you will be able to rest in Him — really rest — and start the next day as a new life."
— St. Teresa Benedicta of the Cross (Edith Stein)

DAY TEN

DATE:

BOOK | CHAPTER | VERSE(S)

PRAY

Come Holy Spirit, fill the hearts of your faithful
and kindle in them the fire of your love.
Send forth your Spirit and they shall be created.
And You shall renew the face of the earth.
O God, who by the light of the Holy Spirit,
did instruct the hearts of the faithful,
grant that by the same Holy Spirit we may be truly wise
and ever enjoy His consolations, Through Christ Our Lord,
Amen.

LECTIO DIVINA

LECTIO

What is the objective meaning of the text?

MEDITATIO

What personal message does the text have for me?

ORATIO

What do I say to the Lord in response to His word?

CONTEMPLATIO

What conversion of mind, heart, and life is He asking of me today?

ACTIO

How will I make my life a gift for others in charity?

What does God want me to do today?

PRAYER PETITIONS

TASKS + TO DOS

MEALS TO NOURISH

KEEPING HOME

KINDNESS TO MYSELF

How did I progress in living the Word today?

"And when night comes,
and you look back over
the day and see how
fragmentary everything
has been, and how much
you planned that has
gone undone, and all
the reasons you have
to be embarrassed
and ashamed: just take
everything exactly as it is,
put it in God's hands and
leave it with Him. Then you
will be able to rest in Him
— really rest — and start
the next day as a new life."
— St. Teresa Benedicta of
the Cross (Edith Stein)

DAY ELEVEN

DATE:

BOOK | CHAPTER | VERSE(S)

PRAY

Come Holy Spirit, fill the hearts of your faithful
and kindle in them the fire of your love.
Send forth your Spirit and they shall be created.
And You shall renew the face of the earth.
O God, who by the light of the Holy Spirit,
did instruct the hearts of the faithful,
grant that by the same Holy Spirit we may be truly wise
and ever enjoy His consolations, Through Christ Our Lord,
Amen.

LECTIO DIVINA

LECTIO

What is the objective meaning
of the text?

MEDITATIO

What personal message does
the text have for me?

ORATIO

What do I say to the Lord in
response to His word?

CONTEMPLATIO

What conversion of mind,
heart, and life is He asking of
me today?

ACTIO

How will I make my life a gift for others in charity?
What does God want me to do today?

PRAYER PETITIONS

TASKS + TO DOS

MEALS TO NOURISH

KEEPING HOME

KINDNESS TO MYSELF

How did I progress in living the Word today?

"And when night comes, and you look back over the day and see how fragmentary everything has been, and how much you planned that has gone undone, and all the reasons you have to be embarrassed and ashamed: just take everything exactly as it is, put it in God's hands and leave it with Him. Then you will be able to rest in Him — really rest — and start the next day as a new life."
— St. Teresa Benedicta of the Cross (Edith Stein)

DAY TWELVE

DATE:

TODAY'S TAKE UP & READ

BOOK | CHAPTER | VERSE(S)

PRAY

Come Holy Spirit, fill the hearts of your faithful
and kindle in them the fire of your love.
Send forth your Spirit and they shall be created.
And You shall renew the face of the earth.
O God, who by the light of the Holy Spirit,
did instruct the hearts of the faithful,
grant that by the same Holy Spirit we may be truly wise
and ever enjoy His consolations, Through Christ Our Lord,
Amen.

LECTIO DIVINA

LECTIO

What is the objective meaning of the text?

MEDITATIO

What personal message does the text have for me?

ORATIO

What do I say to the Lord in response to His word?

CONTEMPLATIO

What conversion of mind, heart, and life is He asking of me today?

How will I make my life a gift for others in charity?

What does God want me to do today?

PRAYER PETITIONS

TASKS + TO DOS

MEALS TO NOURISH

KEEPING HOME

KINDNESS TO MYSELF

How did I progress in living the Word today?

"And when night comes, and you look back over the day and see how fragmentary everything has been, and how much you planned that has gone undone, and all the reasons you have to be embarrassed and ashamed: just take everything exactly as it is, put it in God's hands and leave it with Him. Then you will be able to rest in Him — really rest — and start the next day as a new life."
— St. Teresa Benedicta of the Cross (Edith Stein)

DAY THIRTEEN

DATE:

TODAY'S TAKE UP & READ

BOOK | CHAPTER | VERSE(S)

PRAY

Come Holy Spirit, fill the hearts of your faithful
and kindle in them the fire of your love.
Send forth your Spirit and they shall be created.
And You shall renew the face of the earth.
O God, who by the light of the Holy Spirit,
did instruct the hearts of the faithful,
grant that by the same Holy Spirit we may be truly wise
and ever enjoy His consolations, Through Christ Our Lord,
Amen.

LECTIO DIVINA

LECTIO

What is the objective meaning of the text?

MEDITATIO

What personal message does the text have for me?

ORATIO

What do I say to the Lord in response to His word?

CONTEMPLATIO

What conversion of mind, heart, and life is He asking of me today?

How will I make my life a gift for others in charity?

What does God want me to do today?

PRAYER PETITIONS

TASKS + TO DOS

MEALS TO NOURISH

KEEPING HOME

KINDNESS TO MYSELF

How did I progress in living the Word today?

"And when night comes, and you look back over the day and see how fragmentary everything has been, and how much you planned that has gone undone, and all the reasons you have to be embarrassed and ashamed: just take everything exactly as it is, put it in God's hands and leave it with Him. Then you will be able to rest in Him — really rest — and start the next day as a new life."
— St. Teresa Benedicta of the Cross (Edith Stein)

DAY FOURTEEN

DATE:

TODAY'S TAKE UP & READ

BOOK | CHAPTER | VERSE(S)

PRAY

*Come Holy Spirit, fill the hearts of your faithful
and kindle in them the fire of your love.
Send forth your Spirit and they shall be created.
And You shall renew the face of the earth.
O God, who by the light of the Holy Spirit,
did instruct the hearts of the faithful,
grant that by the same Holy Spirit we may be truly wise
and ever enjoy His consolations, Through Christ Our Lord,
Amen.*

LECTIO DIVINA

LECTIO

What is the objective meaning of the text?

MEDITATIO

What personal message does the text have for me?

ORATIO

What do I say to the Lord in response to His word?

CONTEMPLATIO

What conversion of mind, heart, and life is He asking of me today?

TODAY'S TAKE UP & READ

BOOK | CHAPTER | VERSE(S)

PRAY

Come Holy Spirit, fill the hearts of your faithful
and kindle in them the fire of your love.
Send forth your Spirit and they shall be created.
And You shall renew the face of the earth.
O God, who by the light of the Holy Spirit,
did instruct the hearts of the faithful,
grant that by the same Holy Spirit we may be truly wise
and ever enjoy His consolations, Through Christ Our Lord,
Amen.

LECTIO DIVINA

LECTIO

What is the objective meaning
of the text?

MEDITATIO

What personal message does
the text have for me?

ORATIO

What do I say to the Lord in
response to His word?

CONTEMPLATIO

What conversion of mind,
heart, and life is He asking of
me today?

How did I progress in living the Word today?

"And when night comes, and you look back over the day and see how fragmentary everything has been, and how much you planned that has gone undone, and all the reasons you have to be embarrassed and ashamed: just take everything exactly as it is, put it in God's hands and leave it with Him. Then you will be able to rest in Him — really rest — and start the next day as a new life."
— St. Teresa Benedicta of the Cross (Edith Stein)

DAY FIFTEEN

DATE:

BOOK | CHAPTER | VERSE(S)

WEEKLY SCRIPTURE MEMORY

HIDE IT IN YOUR HEART

When we memorize Scripture, we imitate Jesus, who hid God's Word in His heart and who proclaimed it even in His most sorrowful agony. As He hung in the final moments of His life, Scripture was the last thing on His breath, and Jesus, "crying with a loud voice, said, 'Father, into your hands I commend my spirit.' Having said this, He breathed his last." (Luke 23:46) We can almost certainly know that Jesus learned those words (from Psalm 31) from His mother as a prayer when He was a little boy. She poured into Him a treasury of Scripture and He knew just where to find it all His life.

To hold the Word so close and so dear that it is what sustains us in the very last moments of our life! To hide the Lord in our hearts in such a real and present way that He spills out into our speech when we are neediest and when we are most joyful! These are the true goals of the Take Up & Read studies.

We invite you to use the verses we've chosen in our online Bible reading plans, or to listen to the inspiration of the Holy Spirit and select verses of your own to memorize.

BOOK | CHAPTER | VERSE(S)

P R A Y

Come Holy Spirit, fill the hearts of your faithful
and kindle in them the fire of your love.
Send forth your Spirit and they shall be created.
And You shall renew the face of the earth.
O God, who by the light of the Holy Spirit,
did instruct the hearts of the faithful,
grant that by the same Holy Spirit we may be truly wise
and ever enjoy His consolations, Through Christ Our Lord,
Amen.

LECTIO DIVINA

LECTIO

What is the objective meaning of the text?

MEDITATIO

What personal message does the text have for me?

ORATIO

What do I say to the Lord in response to His word?

CONTEMPLATIO

What conversion of mind, heart, and life is He asking of me today?

ACTIO

How will I make my life a gift for others in charity?
What does God want me to do today?

PRAYER PETITIONS

TASKS + TO DOS

MEALS TO NOURISH

KEEPING HOME

KINDNESS TO MYSELF

How did I progress in living the Word today?

"And when night comes, and you look back over the day and see how fragmentary everything has been, and how much you planned that has gone undone, and all the reasons you have to be embarrassed and ashamed: just take everything exactly as it is, put it in God's hands and leave it with Him. Then you will be able to rest in Him — really rest — and start the next day as a new life."
— St. Teresa Benedicta of the Cross (Edith Stein)

DAY SIXTEEN

DATE:

BOOK | CHAPTER | VERSE(S)

P R A Y

Come Holy Spirit, fill the hearts of your faithful
and kindle in them the fire of your love.
Send forth your Spirit and they shall be created.
And You shall renew the face of the earth.
O God, who by the light of the Holy Spirit,
did instruct the hearts of the faithful,
grant that by the same Holy Spirit we may be truly wise
and ever enjoy His consolations, Through Christ Our Lord,
Amen.

LECTIO DIVINA

LECTIO

What is the objective meaning
of the text?

MEDITATIO

What personal message does
the text have for me?

ORATIO

What do I say to the Lord in
response to His word?

CONTEMPLATIO

What conversion of mind,
heart, and life is He asking of
me today?

ACTIO

How will I make my life a gift for others in charity?

What does God want me to do today?

PRAYER PETITIONS

TASKS + TO DOS

MEALS TO NOURISH

KEEPING HOME

KINDNESS TO MYSELF

How did I progress in living the Word today?

"And when night comes, and you look back over the day and see how fragmentary everything has been, and how much you planned that has gone undone, and all the reasons you have to be embarrassed and ashamed: just take everything exactly as it is, put it in God's hands and leave it with Him. Then you will be able to rest in Him — really rest — and start the next day as a new life."
— St. Teresa Benedicta of the Cross (Edith Stein)

DAY SEVENTEEN

DATE:

BOOK | CHAPTER | VERSE(S)

PRAY

Come Holy Spirit, fill the hearts of your faithful
and kindle in them the fire of your love.
Send forth your Spirit and they shall be created.
And You shall renew the face of the earth.
O God, who by the light of the Holy Spirit,
did instruct the hearts of the faithful,
grant that by the same Holy Spirit we may be truly wise
and ever enjoy His consolations, Through Christ Our Lord,
Amen.

LECTIO DIVINA

LECTIO

What is the objective meaning
of the text?

MEDITATIO

What personal message does
the text have for me?

ORATIO

What do I say to the Lord in
response to His word?

CONTEMPLATIO

What conversion of mind,
heart, and life is He asking of
me today?

ACTIO

How will I make my life a gift for others in charity?

What does God want me to do today?

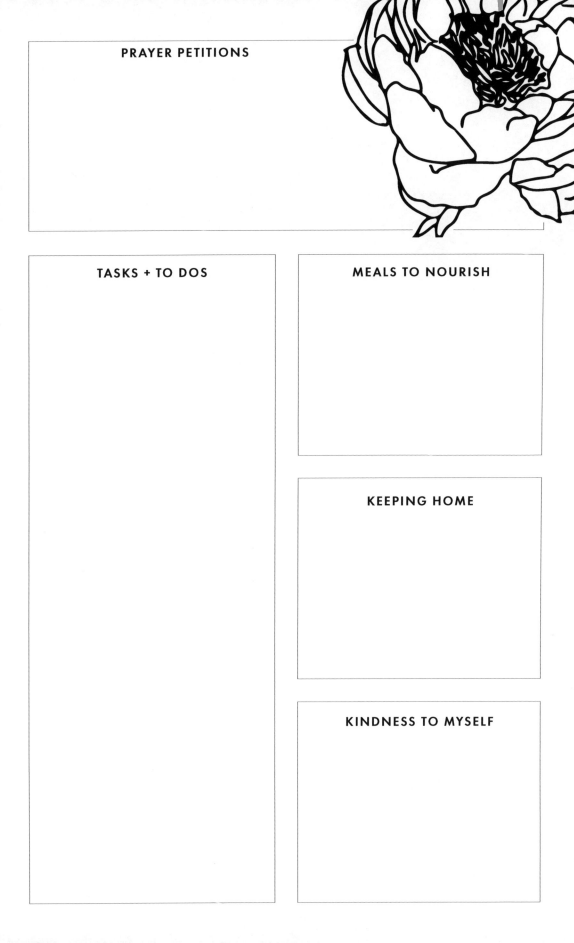

PRAYER PETITIONS

TASKS + TO DOS

MEALS TO NOURISH

KEEPING HOME

KINDNESS TO MYSELF

How did I progress in living the Word today?

"And when night comes, and you look back over the day and see how fragmentary everything has been, and how much you planned that has gone undone, and all the reasons you have to be embarrassed and ashamed: just take everything exactly as it is, put it in God's hands and leave it with Him. Then you will be able to rest in Him — really rest — and start the next day as a new life."
— St. Teresa Benedicta of the Cross (Edith Stein)

DAY EIGHTEEN

DATE:

_____

BOOK | CHAPTER | VERSE(S)

PRAY

Come Holy Spirit, fill the hearts of your faithful
and kindle in them the fire of your love.
Send forth your Spirit and they shall be created.
And You shall renew the face of the earth.
O God, who by the light of the Holy Spirit,
did instruct the hearts of the faithful,
grant that by the same Holy Spirit we may be truly wise
and ever enjoy His consolations, Through Christ Our Lord,
Amen.

LECTIO DIVINA

LECTIO

What is the objective meaning of the text?

MEDITATIO

What personal message does the text have for me?

ORATIO

What do I say to the Lord in response to His word?

CONTEMPLATIO

What conversion of mind, heart, and life is He asking of me today?

ACTIO

How will I make my life a gift for others in charity?
What does God want me to do today?

PRAYER PETITIONS

TASKS + TO DOS

MEALS TO NOURISH

KEEPING HOME

KINDNESS TO MYSELF

How did I progress in living the Word today?

"And when night comes, and you look back over the day and see how fragmentary everything has been, and how much you planned that has gone undone, and all the reasons you have to be embarrassed and ashamed: just take everything exactly as it is, put it in God's hands and leave it with Him. Then you will be able to rest in Him — really rest — and start the next day as a new life."
— St. Teresa Benedicta of the Cross (Edith Stein)

DAY NINETEEN

DATE:

TODAY'S TAKE UP & READ

BOOK | CHAPTER | VERSE(S)

PRAY

Come Holy Spirit, fill the hearts of your faithful
and kindle in them the fire of your love.
Send forth your Spirit and they shall be created.
And You shall renew the face of the earth.
O God, who by the light of the Holy Spirit,
did instruct the hearts of the faithful,
grant that by the same Holy Spirit we may be truly wise
and ever enjoy His consolations, Through Christ Our Lord,
Amen.

LECTIO DIVINA

LECTIO

What is the objective meaning
of the text?

MEDITATIO

What personal message does
the text have for me?

ORATIO

What do I say to the Lord in
response to His word?

CONTEMPLATIO

What conversion of mind,
heart, and life is He asking of
me today?

ACTIO

How will I make my life a gift for others in charity?
What does God want me to do today?

PRAYER PETITIONS

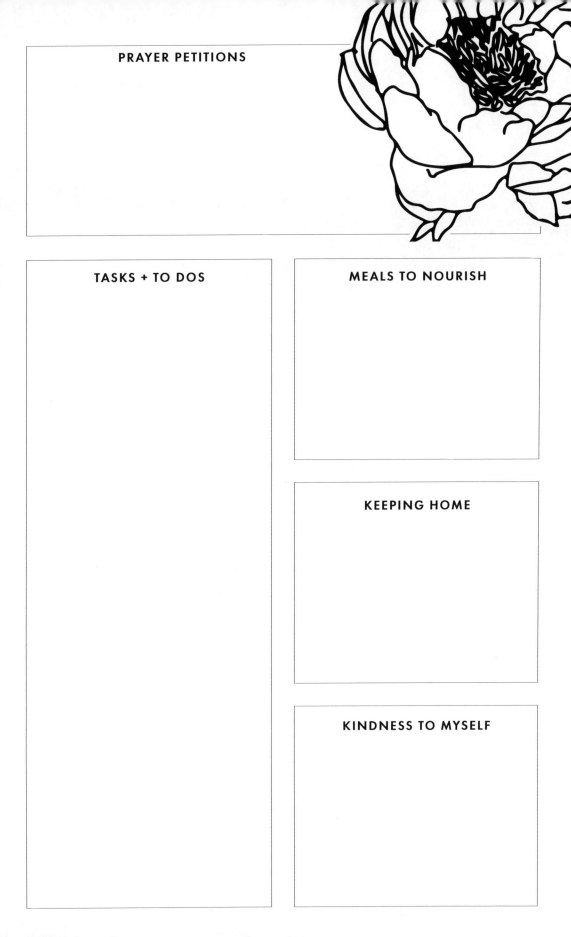

TASKS + TO DOS

MEALS TO NOURISH

KEEPING HOME

KINDNESS TO MYSELF

How did I progress in living the Word today?

"And when night comes, and you look back over the day and see how fragmentary everything has been, and how much you planned that has gone undone, and all the reasons you have to be embarrassed and ashamed: just take everything exactly as it is, put it in God's hands and leave it with Him. Then you will be able to rest in Him — really rest — and start the next day as a new life."
— St. Teresa Benedicta of the Cross (Edith Stein)

DAY TWENTY

DATE:

BOOK | CHAPTER | VERSE(S)

PRAY

Come Holy Spirit, fill the hearts of your faithful
and kindle in them the fire of your love.
Send forth your Spirit and they shall be created.
And You shall renew the face of the earth.
O God, who by the light of the Holy Spirit,
did instruct the hearts of the faithful,
grant that by the same Holy Spirit we may be truly wise
and ever enjoy His consolations, Through Christ Our Lord,

Amen.

LECTIO DIVINA

LECTIO

What is the objective meaning of the text?

MEDITATIO

What personal message does the text have for me?

ORATIO

What do I say to the Lord in response to His word?

CONTEMPLATIO

What conversion of mind, heart, and life is He asking of me today?

ACTIO

How will I make my life a gift for others in charity?
What does God want me to do today?

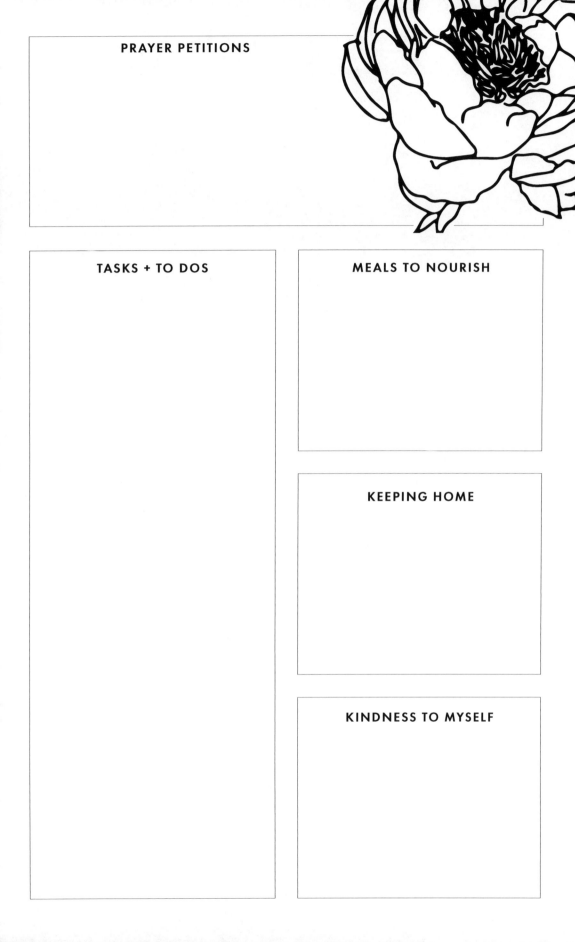

PRAYER PETITIONS

TASKS + TO DOS

MEALS TO NOURISH

KEEPING HOME

KINDNESS TO MYSELF

How did I progress in living the Word today?

"And when night comes, and you look back over the day and see how fragmentary everything has been, and how much you planned that has gone undone, and all the reasons you have to be embarrassed and ashamed: just take everything exactly as it is, put it in God's hands and leave it with Him. Then you will be able to rest in Him — really rest — and start the next day as a new life."
— St. Teresa Benedicta of the Cross (Edith Stein)

DAY TWENTY-ONE

DATE:

BOOK | CHAPTER | VERSE(S)

PRAY

Come Holy Spirit, fill the hearts of your faithful
and kindle in them the fire of your love.
Send forth your Spirit and they shall be created.
And You shall renew the face of the earth.
O God, who by the light of the Holy Spirit,
did instruct the hearts of the faithful,
grant that by the same Holy Spirit we may be truly wise
and ever enjoy His consolations, Through Christ Our Lord,
Amen.

LECTIO DIVINA

LECTIO

What is the objective meaning
of the text?

MEDITATIO

What personal message does
the text have for me?

ORATIO

What do I say to the Lord in
response to His word?

CONTEMPLATIO

What conversion of mind,
heart, and life is He asking of
me today?

ACTIO

How will I make my life a gift for others in charity?
What does God want me to do today?

PRAYER PETITIONS

TASKS + TO DOS

MEALS TO NOURISH

KEEPING HOME

KINDNESS TO MYSELF

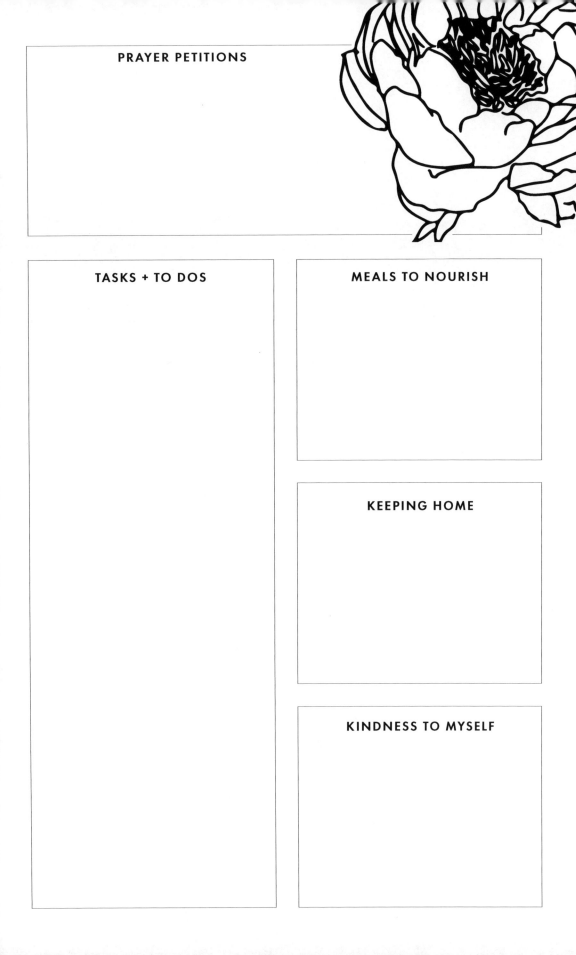

How did I progress in living the Word today?

"And when night comes, and you look back over the day and see how fragmentary everything has been, and how much you planned that has gone undone, and all the reasons you have to be embarrassed and ashamed: just take everything exactly as it is, put it in God's hands and leave it with Him. Then you will be able to rest in Him — really rest — and start the next day as a new life."
— St. Teresa Benedicta of the Cross (Edith Stein)

DAY TWENTY-TWO

DATE:

BOOK | CHAPTER | VERSE(S)

WEEKLY SCRIPTURE MEMORY

HIDE IT IN YOUR HEART

When we memorize Scripture, we imitate Jesus, who hid God's Word in His heart and who proclaimed it even in His most sorrowful agony. As He hung in the final moments of His life, Scripture was the last thing on His breath, and Jesus, "crying with a loud voice, said, 'Father, into your hands I commend my spirit.' Having said this, He breathed his last." (Luke 23:46) We can almost certainly know that Jesus learned those words (from Psalm 31) from His mother as a prayer when He was a little boy. She poured into Him a treasury of Scripture and He knew just where to find it all His life.

To hold the Word so close and so dear that it is what sustains us in the very last moments of our life! To hide the Lord in our hearts in such a real and present way that He spills out into our speech when we are neediest and when we are most joyful! These are the true goals of the Take Up & Read studies.

We invite you to use the verses we've chosen in our online Bible reading plans, or to listen to the inspiration of the Holy Spirit and select verses of your own to memorize.

BOOK | CHAPTER | VERSE(S)

P R A Y

*Come Holy Spirit, fill the hearts of your faithful
and kindle in them the fire of your love.
Send forth your Spirit and they shall be created.
And You shall renew the face of the earth.
O God, who by the light of the Holy Spirit,
did instruct the hearts of the faithful,
grant that by the same Holy Spirit we may be truly wise
and ever enjoy His consolations, Through Christ Our Lord,
Amen.*

LECTIO DIVINA

LECTIO

What is the objective meaning
of the text?

MEDITATIO

What personal message does
the text have for me?

ORATIO

What do I say to the Lord in
response to His word?

CONTEMPLATIO

What conversion of mind,
heart, and life is He asking of
me today?

How will I make my life a gift for others in charity?
What does God want me to do today?

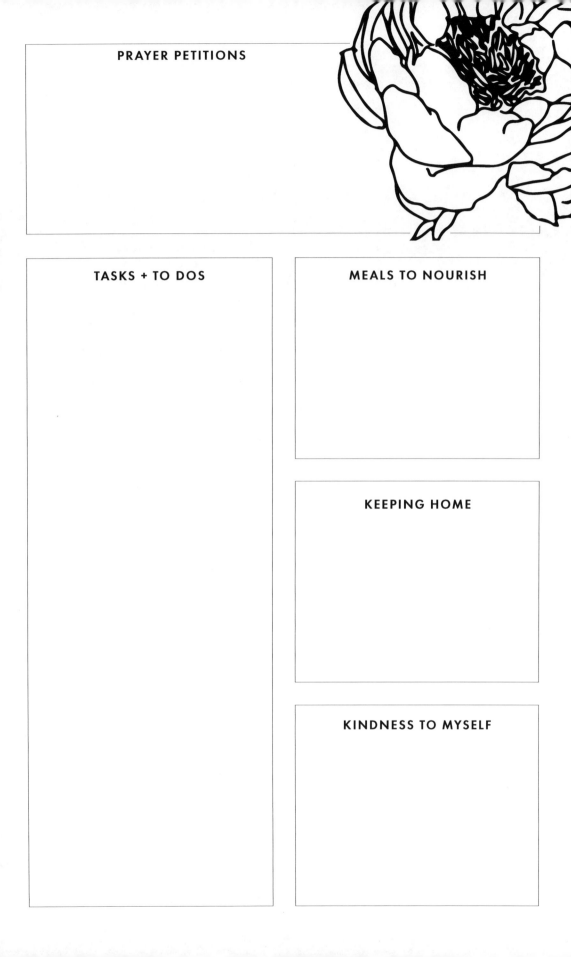

PRAYER PETITIONS

TASKS + TO DOS

MEALS TO NOURISH

KEEPING HOME

KINDNESS TO MYSELF

How did I progress in living the Word today?

"And when night comes, and you look back over the day and see how fragmentary everything has been, and how much you planned that has gone undone, and all the reasons you have to be embarrassed and ashamed: just take everything exactly as it is, put it in God's hands and leave it with Him. Then you will be able to rest in Him — really rest — and start the next day as a new life." — St. Teresa Benedicta of the Cross (Edith Stein)

DAY TWENTY-THREE

DATE:

TODAY'S TAKE UP & READ

BOOK | CHAPTER | VERSE(S)

PRAY

Come Holy Spirit, fill the hearts of your faithful
and kindle in them the fire of your love.
Send forth your Spirit and they shall be created.
And You shall renew the face of the earth.
O God, who by the light of the Holy Spirit,
did instruct the hearts of the faithful,
grant that by the same Holy Spirit we may be truly wise
and ever enjoy His consolations, Through Christ Our Lord,
Amen.

LECTIO DIVINA

LECTIO

What is the objective meaning
of the text?

MEDITATIO

What personal message does
the text have for me?

ORATIO

What do I say to the Lord in
response to His word?

CONTEMPLATIO

What conversion of mind,
heart, and life is He asking of
me today?

ACTIO

How will I make my life a gift for others in charity?

What does God want me to do today?

PRAYER PETITIONS

TASKS + TO DOS

MEALS TO NOURISH

KEEPING HOME

KINDNESS TO MYSELF

How did I progress in living the Word today?

"And when night comes, and you look back over the day and see how fragmentary everything has been, and how much you planned that has gone undone, and all the reasons you have to be embarrassed and ashamed: just take everything exactly as it is, put it in God's hands and leave it with Him. Then you will be able to rest in Him — really rest — and start the next day as a new life."
— St. Teresa Benedicta of the Cross (Edith Stein)

DAY TWENTY-FOUR

DATE:

BOOK | CHAPTER | VERSE(S)

PRAY

Come Holy Spirit, fill the hearts of your faithful
and kindle in them the fire of your love.
Send forth your Spirit and they shall be created.
And You shall renew the face of the earth.
O God, who by the light of the Holy Spirit,
did instruct the hearts of the faithful,
grant that by the same Holy Spirit we may be truly wise
and ever enjoy His consolations, Through Christ Our Lord,
Amen.

LECTIO DIVINA

LECTIO

What is the objective meaning
of the text?

MEDITATIO

What personal message does
the text have for me?

ORATIO

What do I say to the Lord in
response to His word?

CONTEMPLATIO

What conversion of mind,
heart, and life is He asking of
me today?

ACTIO

How will I make my life a gift for others in charity?
What does God want me to do today?

PRAYER PETITIONS

TASKS + TO DOS

MEALS TO NOURISH

KEEPING HOME

KINDNESS TO MYSELF

How did I progress in living the Word today?

"And when night comes, and you look back over the day and see how fragmentary everything has been, and how much you planned that has gone undone, and all the reasons you have to be embarrassed and ashamed: just take everything exactly as it is, put it in God's hands and leave it with Him. Then you will be able to rest in Him — really rest — and start the next day as a new life."
— St. Teresa Benedicta of the Cross (Edith Stein)

DAY TWENTY-FIVE

DATE:

BOOK | CHAPTER | VERSE(S)

PRAY

Come Holy Spirit, fill the hearts of your faithful
and kindle in them the fire of your love.
Send forth your Spirit and they shall be created.
And You shall renew the face of the earth.
O God, who by the light of the Holy Spirit,
did instruct the hearts of the faithful,
grant that by the same Holy Spirit we may be truly wise
and ever enjoy His consolations, Through Christ Our Lord,
Amen.

LECTIO DIVINA

LECTIO

What is the objective meaning of the text?

MEDITATIO

What personal message does the text have for me?

ORATIO

What do I say to the Lord in response to His word?

CONTEMPLATIO

What conversion of mind, heart, and life is He asking of me today?

ACTIO

How will I make my life a gift for others in charity?
What does God want me to do today?

PRAYER PETITIONS

TASKS + TO DOS

MEALS TO NOURISH

KEEPING HOME

KINDNESS TO MYSELF

How did I progress in living the Word today?

"And when night comes, and you look back over the day and see how fragmentary everything has been, and how much you planned that has gone undone, and all the reasons you have to be embarrassed and ashamed: just take everything exactly as it is, put it in God's hands and leave it with Him. Then you will be able to rest in Him — really rest — and start the next day as a new life."
— St. Teresa Benedicta of the Cross (Edith Stein)

DAY TWENTY-SIX

DATE:

BOOK | CHAPTER | VERSE(S)

P R A Y

Come Holy Spirit, fill the hearts of your faithful
and kindle in them the fire of your love.
Send forth your Spirit and they shall be created.
And You shall renew the face of the earth.
O God, who by the light of the Holy Spirit,
did instruct the hearts of the faithful,
grant that by the same Holy Spirit we may be truly wise
and ever enjoy His consolations, Through Christ Our Lord,
Amen.

LECTIO DIVINA

LECTIO

What is the objective meaning of the text?

MEDITATIO

What personal message does the text have for me?

ORATIO

What do I say to the Lord in response to His word?

CONTEMPLATIO

What conversion of mind, heart, and life is He asking of me today?

ACTIO

How will I make my life a gift for others in charity?

What does God want me to do today?

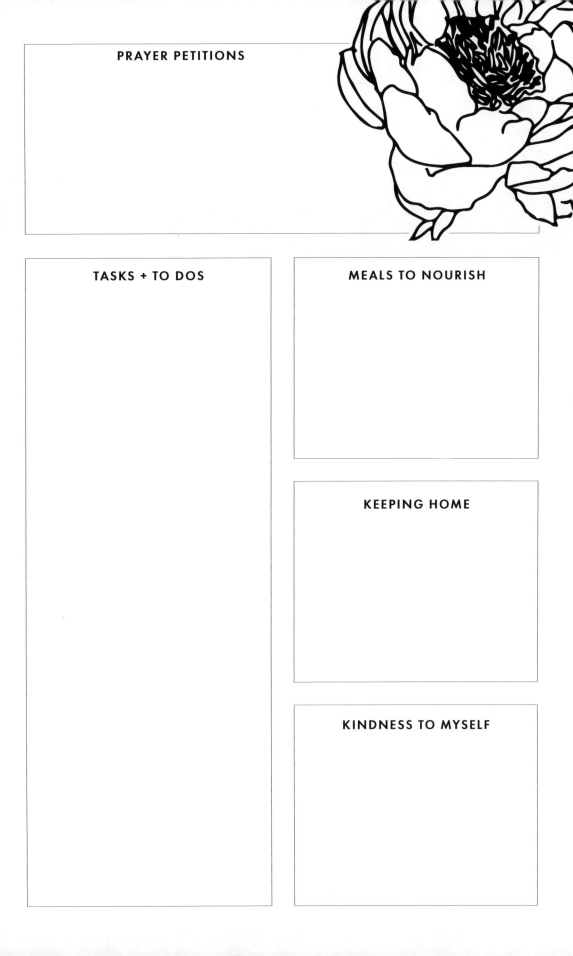

PRAYER PETITIONS

TASKS + TO DOS

MEALS TO NOURISH

KEEPING HOME

KINDNESS TO MYSELF

How did I progress in living the Word today?

"And when night comes, and you look back over the day and see how fragmentary everything has been, and how much you planned that has gone undone, and all the reasons you have to be embarrassed and ashamed: just take everything exactly as it is, put it in God's hands and leave it with Him. Then you will be able to rest in Him — really rest — and start the next day as a new life."
— St. Teresa Benedicta of the Cross (Edith Stein)

DAY TWENTY-SEVEN

DATE:

TODAY'S TAKE UP & READ

BOOK | CHAPTER | VERSE(S)

PRAY

Come Holy Spirit, fill the hearts of your faithful
and kindle in them the fire of your love.
Send forth your Spirit and they shall be created.
And You shall renew the face of the earth.
O God, who by the light of the Holy Spirit,
did instruct the hearts of the faithful,
grant that by the same Holy Spirit we may be truly wise
and ever enjoy His consolations, Through Christ Our Lord,

Amen.

LECTIO DIVINA

LECTIO

What is the objective meaning
of the text?

MEDITATIO

What personal message does
the text have for me?

ORATIO

What do I say to the Lord in
response to His word?

CONTEMPLATIO

What conversion of mind,
heart, and life is He asking of
me today?

How will I make my life a gift for others in charity?
What does God want me to do today?

PRAYER PETITIONS

TASKS + TO DOS

MEALS TO NOURISH

KEEPING HOME

KINDNESS TO MYSELF

How did I progress in living the Word today?

"And when night comes, and you look back over the day and see how fragmentary everything has been, and how much you planned that has gone undone, and all the reasons you have to be embarrassed and ashamed: just take everything exactly as it is, put it in God's hands and leave it with Him. Then you will be able to rest in Him — really rest — and start the next day as a new life."
— St. Teresa Benedicta of the Cross (Edith Stein)

DAY TWENTY-EIGHT

DATE:

TODAY'S TAKE UP & READ

BOOK | CHAPTER | VERSE(S)

PRAY

Come Holy Spirit, fill the hearts of your faithful
and kindle in them the fire of your love.
Send forth your Spirit and they shall be created.
And You shall renew the face of the earth.
O God, who by the light of the Holy Spirit,
did instruct the hearts of the faithful,
grant that by the same Holy Spirit we may be truly wise
and ever enjoy His consolations, Through Christ Our Lord,
Amen.

LECTIO DIVINA

LECTIO

What is the objective meaning
of the text?

MEDITATIO

What personal message does
the text have for me?

ORATIO

What do I say to the Lord in
response to His word?

CONTEMPLATIO

What conversion of mind,
heart, and life is He asking of
me today?

ACTIO

How will I make my life a gift for others in charity?
What does God want me to do today?

PRAYER PETITIONS

TASKS + TO DOS

MEALS TO NOURISH

KEEPING HOME

KINDNESS TO MYSELF

END DATE

CLOSING PRAYER

Made in the USA
Lexington, KY
10 April 2018